JESSICA ENNIS

Roy

Illustrated by Chris King

First published in 2012 by
Franklin Watts
338 Euston Road
London NW1 3BH

Franklin Watts Australia
Level 17/207 Kent Street
Sydney NSW 2000

Text © Roy Apps 2012
Illustrations © Chris King 2012
Cover design by Peter Scoulding

A CIP catalogue record for this book
is available from the British Library.

ISBN: 978 1 4451 1832 1

1 3 5 7 9 10 8 6 4 2

Printed in Great Britain

Franklin Watts is a division of Hachette Children's Books,
an Hachette UK company.
www.hachette.co.uk

Chapter One:
First Prize

Jess sat looking out of the kitchen window. She was bored. It was the middle of the summer holidays and there was nothing to do. It was ages until her favourite TV programme,

Junior Masterchef, came on at teatime. When she left school, Jess was going to become a chef. She loved cooking. Her dad was always cooking the most amazing West Indian dishes.

Jess's mum came into the kitchen. "What are you going to do today, Jess?" she asked.

Jess shrugged. "Dunno."

"Why don't you go to that holiday athletics club they told you about at school? I'm sure you'd enjoy it. You're good at PE."

"None of my mates are going," said Jess. "I won't know anyone there."

"You can take Carmel," replied her mum.

Jess groaned. A whole afternoon in a strange holiday club with her little sister? It didn't sound like much fun.

"No arguments," said Jess's mum, cheerily. "I'm not having you under my feet all day. I'll run you both down to the Don Valley Stadium in the car."

At the stadium Carmel soon found some of her mates and went off with them. Jess was left on her own, surrounded by a lot of other children who had turned up. One of the athletics club organisers came up to her.

"Hi there! Would you like to try hurdling?"

Jess shrugged.

"There's a prize for the best hurdler at the end of the week," the organiser told her. "A pair of sports trainers."

Jess stared at the trainers. They were the smartest, coolest trainers she had ever seen. She knew her mum and dad would never be able to afford to buy her trainers like that. Suddenly, Jess's mind was made up. She would come to the club every day, practise her hurdling and win those trainers.

But when it came to the final hurdle race, Jess found herself feeling nervous. She'd heard somebody say, "Who's that skinny kid?" She knew it was true. She was the smallest competitor on the track, and just ten years old.

Once the race began though, nothing else mattered. Jess simply flew over the hurdles. She won the race easily. After she picked up her prize, one of the athletics coaches came over. He handed a sheet of paper to Jess. "Have you been hurdling long?" he asked.

"Just this week," Jess replied. The coach looked stunned.

Back at home, Jess stuck her winner's certificate onto her bedroom wall. She gave her dad the paper from the coach. It was an invitation for her to join the City of Sheffield Athletic Club Young Athletes, at the Don Valley Stadium.

Jess carefully put her brand-new trainers in the bottom of her wardrobe. She would wear them next time she went to the athletics club. There was no doubt at all in her mind; she was going to become an athlete.

Chapter Two:

The School Record

In 1997, the year after Jess won her
trainers, she started secondary school.
She liked it there. The teachers were
friendly and in PE she did proper
athletics.

The running track wasn't up to much though. It was wet and boggy. Then her PE teacher, Mr Eccles, said to her, "Ever thought of trying the high jump, Jess? You won't get so muddy over there."

Jess enjoyed the high jump and carried on practising it throughout the summer term. Each week, Mr Eccles raised the bar higher and higher.

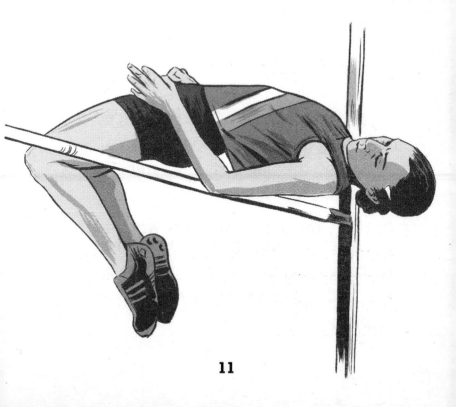

At the end of term, it was the Sheffield Schools Athletics Championships. Jess was entered for the high jump. With each successful jump the officials raised the bar, until it reached 1.56 metres.

Mr Eccles came over to her. "Do you think you can clear that, Jess? If you can, it will be a Sheffield schools' record."

Jess nodded. She looked at the bar. It did look quite high. She ran, sprang and jumped. She just cleared it!

When she got up, Mr Eccles bounced over with a huge smile on his face. "Stand by the bar, Jess. I'm going to take a photo," he said.

Mr Eccles's photo showed just how amazing the jump had been. The bar Jess had cleared to set a new schools' record was taller than she was!

After school, at weekends and during the holidays, Jess continued her training with the City of Sheffield Athletic Club. By the time she was fifteen, she regularly entered Under 20 events. It was great doing something she enjoyed, but it wasn't easy. After school she did her homework and had something to eat. Then her mum or dad drove her over to the track. Jess wasn't getting home until nine o'clock. There was just time for a bit of pasta, before going to bed.

As a fifteen-year-old, Jess ran in the trials for the Great Britain Under 20's team. She managed to come third, which was great, but not good enough to get her selected for the team. She couldn't help feeling disappointed.

At the end of the race, her mum came over to her. "You did so well, Jess," she said. "The girls you were racing against

were all three or four years older than you. You just wait until you're eighteen or nineteen. You're sure to get into the national team then."

Jess knew her mum was right, but it still didn't help her feel any better. It would be years before she was eighteen. Deep down, she wondered if she could really keep up all the hard work — all the training — until then.

Chapter Three:

National Team

A few weeks later, Jess was in a class, when her PE teacher, Mr Eccles, came in. He whispered something to the class teacher.

"Jess," said the teacher. "Pack up your work. Mr Eccles needs a word with you."

Outside in the corridor, Mr Eccles said, "You know the GB Under 20's trials, where you came third? The girl who came second — who was selected for the GB team — has had to pull out. They've asked you to take her place."

Jess could hardly believe her ears.

"You mean I'm in the girls' Under 20's national team?"

"That's right," replied Mr Eccles. "They want you for the next international event in Bedford."

Several months later, in the car on the way down to Bedford, Jess asked her mum, "Do you think the others will think it's a bit, you know... funny? Me being there when I'm only fifteen?"

"Of course not," her mum replied. "You're there as part of the GB team, the same as all the others."

Jess's mum was right. When Jess got trackside, she didn't feel any different to the others. Sure, Jess was a bit shorter, but everyone was in the same team, wearing the GB vest. Nobody treated her like a school kid. She felt like a real athlete. She enjoyed the excitement of the competition and by the time she got back home to Sheffield, she knew exactly what she wanted to do.

"I want to go to the Olympics in 2008," she told her coach, Tony Minichiello.

He grinned. "There's no reason you shouldn't," he replied. "But nobody should just want to go to the Olympics. You should be wanting to go there to win a medal!"

Jess laughed. "OK!" she said. "I want to go to the 2008 Olympics and win a medal!"

It didn't take Jess long to become a top British Junior. She was good at both running and jumping, and concentrated on the heptathlon. This is a really tough discipline, where athletes complete seven different events: 100 metres hurdles, high jump, shot put, 200 metres, long jump, javelin and 800 metres. Each athlete is awarded points depending on how well they perform in each event.

At the 2006 Commonwealth Games, when Jess was 20 years old, she won a bronze medal. Two years later she was picked by Team GB to go to the Beijing Olympics.

Nothing could stop her now.

Chapter Four:

Disaster!

Jess's mum ran into the kitchen. She was waving an envelope in her hand.

"The tickets have come!" she yelled, excitedly.

Jess's mum and dad were going to Beijing to see her perform in the 2008 Olympic Games. They had used all of their savings to pay for the flights and hotels.

"That's great, Mum!" said Jess, giving her mum a hug. "I've got to dash. I mustn't be late for training." Jess picked up her bag and ran out of the house, slamming the front door behind her. Her mum laughed. Jess was always in such a hurry. Still, that was no bad thing, she thought to herself, if like Jess, you were going to be an Olympic athlete.

Jess was taking part in a series of events to prepare her for the Beijing Olympics. In June 2008, she was in Austria, taking part in her last heptathlon competition before she flew out to Beijing.

On day one of the heptathlon, Jess ran really well in the 100 metres hurdles. Then during the high jump she felt a slight pain in her foot. She had some treatment and it seemed to go away.

In the next event — the shot put — Jess posted a personal best score. This moved her up into second place. Her preparations for the Olympics were going as planned.

It was during the 200 metres, one of her strongest events, that Jess knew something was definitely wrong with her foot. As she was coming into the finishing straight, it was as if her legs had suddenly filled with concrete. She just couldn't push away for the final spurt.

At the finishing line she collapsed onto the ground. Her right foot felt like it was on fire.

Jess tried to stand up, but fell to the ground again.

She knew the injury was bad, but she had no idea that it would almost destroy her dreams.

Chapter Five:

Learning to Walk Again

The doctor's face was grim. He clipped some X-rays onto a board on the wall. Then he looked down at Jess, who was lying on a treatment bed.

"You have a triple stress fracture in your foot," he explained. "That means three small bones have been broken owing to the pressure that has been put on them with all your running and jumping."

"That's serious, isn't it?" Jess said, quietly.

The doctor nodded. "At best, you're going to be out of athletics for a year or more..." His voice trailed off.

Jess didn't want to ask, but she knew she had to. "And at worst?" she whispered.

"I'm sorry, Jess. You may not be able to take part in competitive athletics again," the doctor replied.

Jess closed her eyes. She tried to take in what the doctor had just told her. Suddenly, she felt very upset, very angry — and very frightened. All the hard work, all the training, all the looking forward to taking part in the Beijing Olympics. Had it all really been for nothing? Was her career going to end at the age of twenty-two, just as she was about to hit peak form?

The truth was, no one knew the answer to that. Whether Jess still had a future in competitive athletics or not depended entirely on how she responded to treatment.

Every day for an hour Jess had to lie on a magnetic bed. Twice a day for twenty minutes she had to use a special Exogen machine which, using ultrasound, would help her broken bones to heal. She had to wear a protective boot for two whole months.

Jess responded well to the treatment, but she still had a long way to go.

"What you've got to remember, Jess, is this," her physiotherapist told her, "you've not been able to use your foot for months. The bones have healed nicely, but they are fragile. When we get you back onto your feet, it will be like having to learn to walk all over again."

Once she could stand again, with the help of her physio, Jess took it — literally — one step at a time.

Jess's mum and dad helped and encouraged her. Jess felt bad that they had spent all their savings on flights and hotels for the Beijing Olympics, which of course, she'd had to withdraw from.

One day, she promised herself, they'd be able to watch her win an Olympic medal. She was going to make sure of that.

Chapter Six:

Back on Track

The treatment and the exercise paid off. Incredibly, just a year after her serious injury, Jess was back taking part in competitive athletics.

At the 2009 World Athletics Championships in Berlin, Jess won gold in the heptathlon, notching up a personal best score of 6,587 points. The joy she felt when she was presented with the winner's medal was tinged with sadness, though. She had really wanted her mum and dad to be there to see her triumph, but they hadn't got the money for the trip.

It made Jess even more determined to train hard so that she would perform well at the next Olympic Games, in London 2012. After all, London was one place her mum and dad would have no difficulty in getting to.

Over the next two-and-a-half years, Jess continued to do well. She won the heptathlon gold medal at the 2010 European Championships with another personal best score. This time it was also a European Championship Record score: 6,823 points.

At the 2012 World Indoor Athletics Championships in Turkey, Jess achieved yet another personal best score: but she only came second. She knew she still had work to do.

An event in Manchester, just a couple of months before the London Olympics, looked a good place for Jess to show that she was the best. In the 100 metres hurdles, she set off at a cracking pace.

She won the race in 12.75 seconds: another personal best time.

As Jess smiled to the crowd at the finishing line, she couldn't help feeling that there had been something a bit odd about the race. She turned back towards the track and saw the officials in a huddle, talking together. They were looking at the hurdles. Jess and the other competitors looked, too.

Suddenly, she realised why the race had felt strange. The organisers hadn't put out enough hurdles! There were only nine, instead of the regulation ten!

Jess knew what would happen now. It was inevitable. The race was declared void, and Jess's personal best time was erased from the record books. She felt angry and let down.

"How could they put out the wrong number of hurdles?" she asked Tony, her coach, as he tried to comfort her. "Even at school they knew how many hurdles to put out!"

Chapter Seven:
Gold!

Jess trained hard, right up to the
London Olympics. Everyone was
saying she could win gold; everyone
wanted her — the Team GB poster
girl — to get gold. But would she?

Or would the pressure tell?

The first event was the 100 metres hurdles. As Jess jogged out onto the track, she couldn't help but count the number of hurdles.

The starting pistol was fired and the athletes sprinted down the track. Once again, Jess led the field and crossed the line in first place. Another personal best time, and this time the record stood.

By the time the competitors began to take their marks for the final event, the 800 metres, Jess knew that with 5,971 points already, Olympic gold was almost hers. She didn't need to win the final race. The spectators knew this, too.
As she emerged onto the track, a huge roar went up from the home crowd.

Of course, Jess could have taken it easy. But there was something special about competing in London at the Olympics. For the final time in the competition, she took her place on the starting line, still the smallest figure on the track.

Jess took an early lead, but on the back straight Lilli Schwarzkopf of Germany and Tatyana Chernova of Russia overtook her. As they ran into the final straight, Jess powered forward to the delight of the 80,000-strong crowd. She raced across the finishing line in first place.

Jess's final score of 6,955 points was another personal best, and a British and Commonwealth record.

This time her parents were there to see her. As she collected her gold medal, to a huge roar from the crowd, Jessica Ennis already knew what she would do with it. She'd take it back to her home in Sheffield and keep it with her other great treasure — the certificate she won at the Don Valley Stadium, back when she was just ten years old.

Fact file
Jessica Ennis

Full name: Jessica Ennis

Born: 28 January 1986, Sheffield, England

Height: 1.65 metres

Club: City of Sheffield Athletic Club

Major Medals

- **2004 Commonwealth Youth Games**
  Silver, 100m hurdles
  Silver, High Jump

- **2005 European Junior Championships**
  Gold, Heptathlon

- **2006 Commonwealth Games**
  Bronze, Heptathlon

- **2007 European Cup**
  Gold, Heptathlon

- **2009 World Championships**
  Gold, Heptathlon

- **2010 World Indoor Championships**
  Gold, Pentathlon

- **2011 World Championships**
  Silver, Heptathlon

- **2012 World Indoor Championships**
  Silver, Pentathlon

- **2012 Olympic Games**
  Gold, Heptathlon

Other Achievements and Honours

- **2011** Created a member of the Order of the British Empire (MBE).
- **2012** British and Commonwealth record score in heptathlon of 6,955 points.
- **2012** Voted British Athlete of the Year in a public poll run by UK Athletics.
- **2012** Sheffield United Football Club announces that the Bramall Lane stand will be renamed The Jessica Ennis Stand.
- **2012** Featured on special Olympic edition of the *Beano* comic as 'Ennis the Menace'!

DREAM TO WIN

Bradley Wiggins

Bradley and his mum watched as the two riders sped round the cycle track. One bike stood out — it looked like something from a sci-fi movie. The rider's helmet was weird, too. It had a long point at the back going all the way down his neck. But the cyclist on the sci-fi bike soon powered past reigning world champion, Jens Lehmann.

"And it's gold for Chris Boardman, and for Great Britain!" screamed the commentator.

While his mum leapt around the room, whooping with delight, Bradley sat there staring at the TV. He couldn't take his eyes off Chris Boardman and his amazing Lotus super machine.

Bradley Wiggins was twelve years old, and he was hooked on bikes...

Continue reading this story in:
DREAM TO WIN:
Bradley Wiggins